Red Across Kosciusko County
2012
It's your time to climb!
— Jeb Hilbury

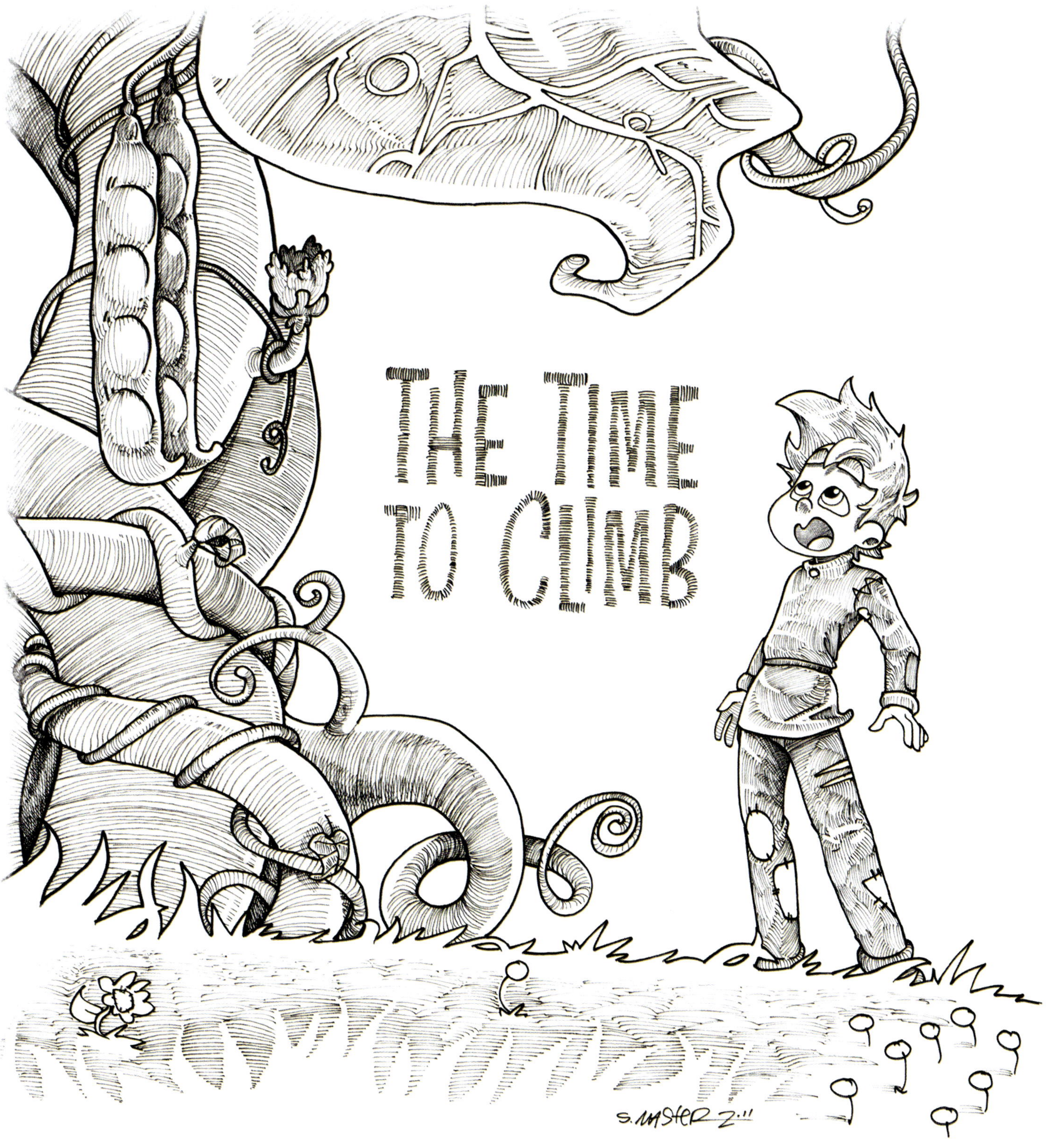
THE TIME
TO CLIMB
S. MASTER 2.'11

The Time To Climb
© 2012 Joel Hilchey
All rights reserved.
ISBN 978-0-9849402-0-2

"This book may have been written for kids, but it should be read by everyone."
-Toni Newman, Strategic Innovation Catalyst

Written by Joel Hilchey
Illustrated by Sebastian Jaster

Printed by Signature Book Printing
www.sbpbooks.com
First printing, January 2012
Printed in the USA

Join the adventure at
www.thetimetoclimb.com

To everyone who has ever taken a chance...

Come listen, my friends, there's a tale to be told
Of a young boy's adventures, of beanstalks and gold.
Come on! Take a chance, and let's see how things grow
This story's for YOU, so get ready, set, go!

Not so long ago and not so far away,
In a land quite like yours at the end of the day,
A young boy named Jack and his mother did sit
In a shib-shabby shack that was just dimly lit.

The cupboards and garden were empty throughout,
You see all that would grow was a lone Brussels sprout.

So, hungry, they sat. Mother cried with a sigh:
"You must go sell our cow!" And a tear filled Jack's eye.

She gave milk every day, their old cow, Milky White,
And though life wasn't fancy, she liked it alright.
She passed her time well: She spent most time out mooing,
And eating and chewing and peeing and .. wooing.

Milky White was Jack's friend, but the family was stuck.
They needed the cash; they were down on their luck.
Though they once had had lots, the two now had much less.
It could happen to anyone out there, I guess.

Nervous Jack took his cow, new adventures to find,
His frown turned around by his positive mind.

And a funny thing happened when Jack lost his fear ...

The world, it seemed brighter, the path became clear.

Jack walked on in style and his confidence grew,
He was hip, he was with it, and liking it too!

Just then, an odd creature appeared on Jack's way - Jack knew by his smile that his heart was okay.

He held out his hand and then winked his left eye.
"An adventure, seek you, and a cow do seek I !
The cow you do have, and these five beans have I.
Plant the beans, climb the beanstalk, and you'll reach the sky!
It's YOUR choice of course, to accept or refuse.
I can offer the beans, but it's YOU who must choose."

Jack longed for adventure, and Jack's time was now!
So the trade he accepted, the beans for his cow.
A cow for some beans? T'was a trade quite absurd!
But the story ends well, as you've probably heard.

So Jack hurried home,
magic beans in his hand,
But his mother, he feared,
would not quite understand.

And angry she was: Mother yelled, screamed and jumped!
She hollered and pounded and hooted and thumped!

But understand this: See when times they are tough,
Though it seldom does good, people sometimes get rough.

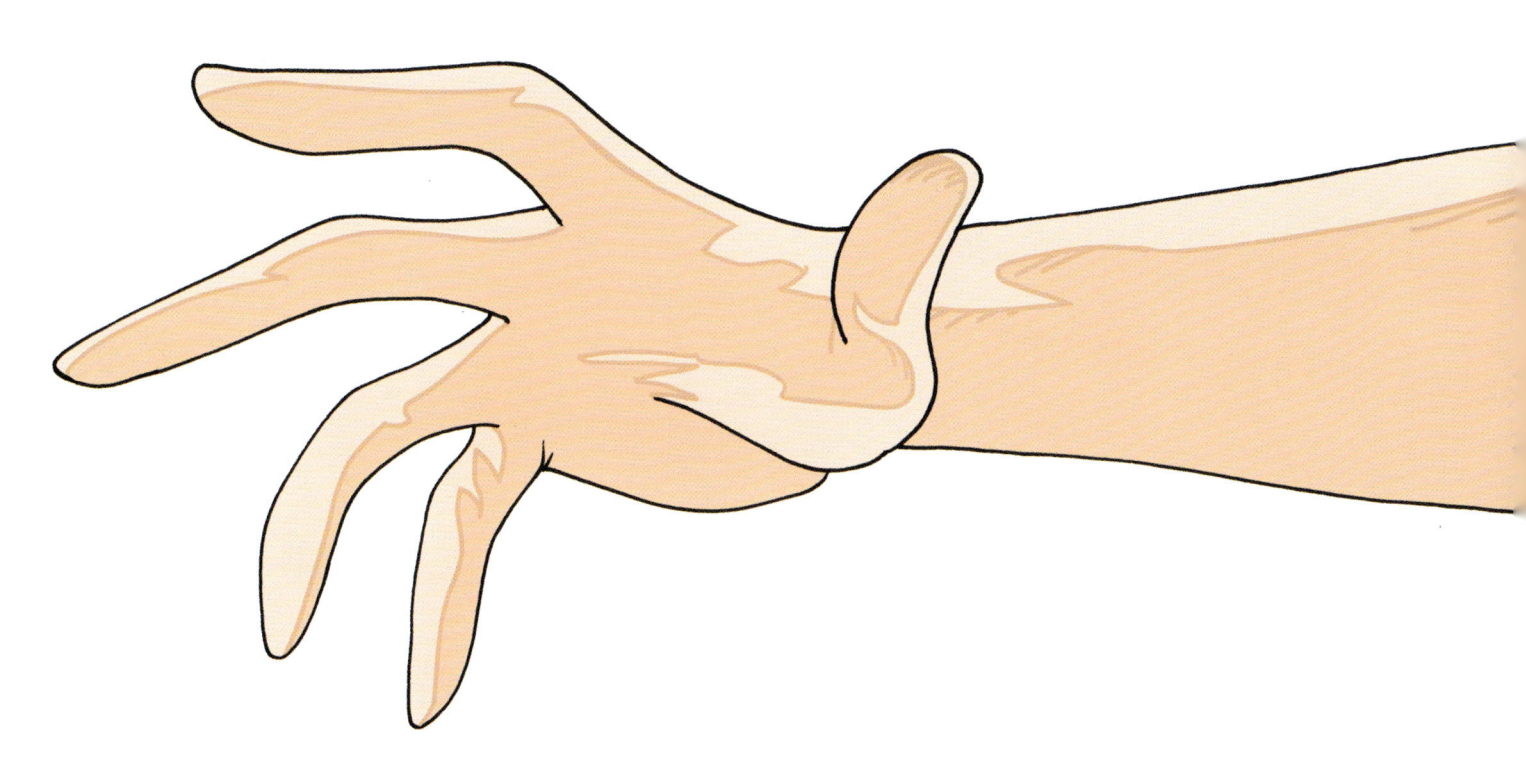

Jack's mom sometimes threw things when not quite content,
So those five magic beans, out the window they went!

Now things may seem bad,
but 'tis often the case
That the spot the beans fall
is the spot-on right place!

That fellow spoke truth, for 'twas when morning came
That the light through Jack's window was not quite the same.

A beanstalk grew tall;
it grew clear to the sky!
Jack had taken a chance,
and now Jack could see why!

It was Jack's time to climb!
But it looked awfully high.
He stared up at his goal -
at the cloud in the sky.

Would our friend Jack succeed?
Could he make it that high?
Jack knew he'd not know ..
'til he gave it a try.

So Jack started to climb,
scrambled high off the ground -
His eyes opened wide as he looked all around!
There were beak-tweeters, buzz-bizzers,
flit-flaps and more!

There were views he'd not even imagined before! He'd once thought this place boring, but Jack had been wrong.

Was it true? Was this how it had been all along?

Jack kept right on climbing up, up, even higher!
But just part way up, Jack then.. started to. . . tire.
The climb was quite hard - this was no easy task,
But if Jack would go on, 'twas *himself* he must ask.

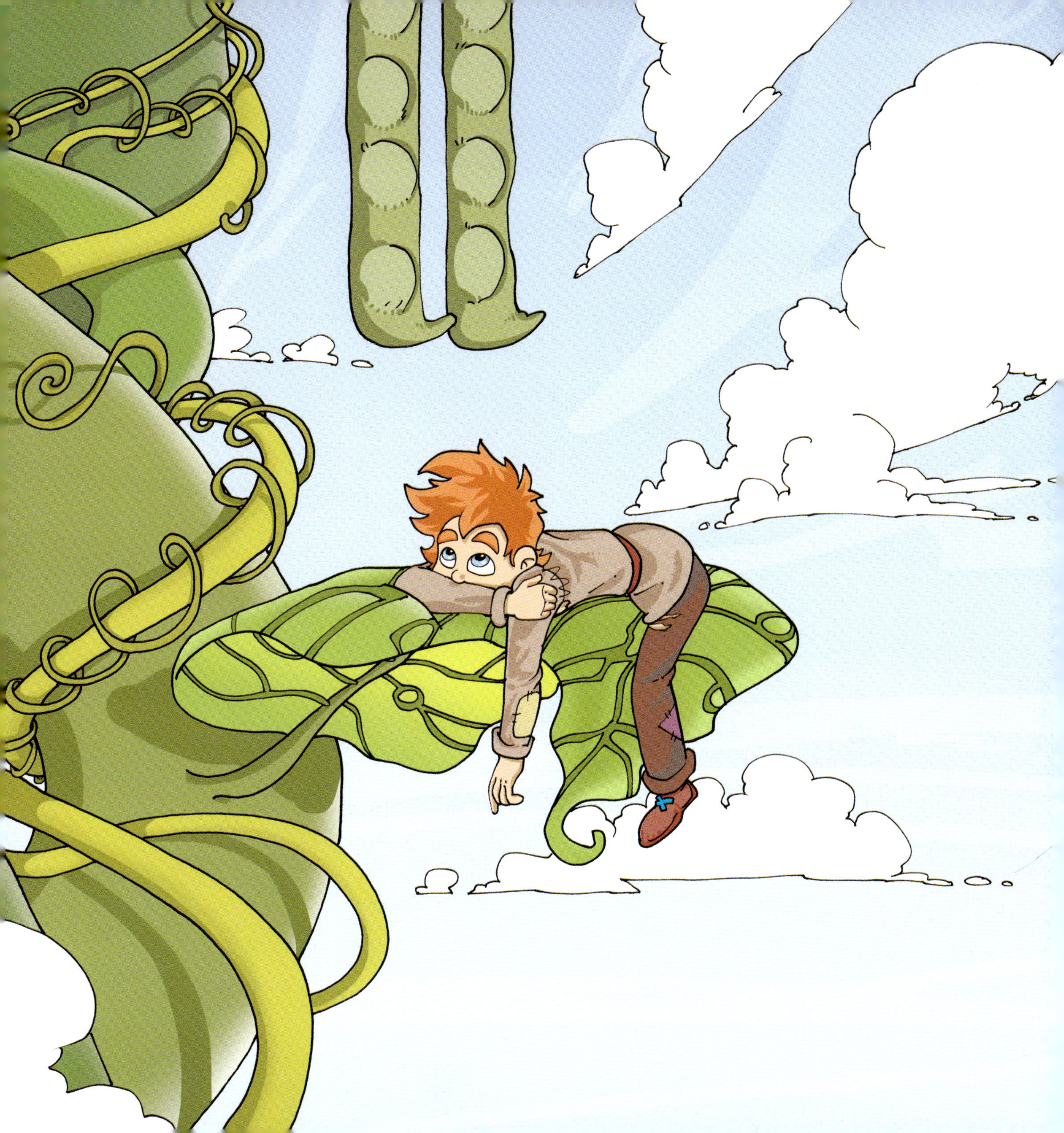

The end of this story
I'm *not* going to tell.
YOU decide for yourself whether
Jack will fare well.

You see, Jack's just a symbol, but YOUR life is real!
Why not find your own **Beanstalk**, then see how you feel?
You can set your own goals, climb for power or wealth,
Or choose friendship or family or travel or health!

But choose wisely, my friends,
for you just may succeed,
And this story has something to teach us, indeed!
Amongst giants and gold,
I would still make the claim.
It was climbing the beanstalk that earned Jack his fame!

You see, happiness
isn't about just the ends:
It's the journey, adventure,
your family and friends!
Your life is YOUR story,
so NOW is your time,
Take a chance on
those beans...

... It's YOUR time to climb!